# F*CK THAT CAPE

*The Grown Woman's Unapologetic Guide to Putting Herself First*

*By*

JENNIFER ARNISE

## FOLLOW JENNIFER ARNISE

Website
jenniferarnise.com

Facebook
jenniferarnise.com/facebook

Instagram
instagram.com/iamjenniferarnise

Twitter
@jenniferarnise

# FUCK THAT CAPE

## THE GROWN WOMAN'S UNAPOLOGETIC GUIDE TO PUTTING HERSELF FIRST

JENNIFER ARNISE

Published 2018

Cover design by Jennifer Arnise

Book design by Jennifer Arnise

Arnise, Jennifer, 1974-

F*ck That Cape: The Grown Woman's Unapologetic Guide to Putting Herself First / Jennifer Arnise

Trade paper **ISBN**: 978-0-692-08139-6

1. Goal (Psychology) 2. Self-realization.

# DEDICATION

*To my best friend and son Vincent. I have learned so much from you. Thank you.*

# TABLE OF CONTENTS

# CHAPTER I

## THE LOVE LETTER

When I first started telling people that my mission was to make Black women remember how beautiful and valuable and truly powerful they are I was met with a lot of resistance, from black folks. They said I could make more money if I catered to all women and that the pool of Black women would be too small to make an impact. I thought about their advice and could understand their logic. Then I thought about all the things that were made for all women. Everything ever made for ALL women were never made for Black women. I remembered how it felt not having my story as a woman of color told in books about healing, the mental and emotional effects of trauma, and forget about opening any magazine in the grocery store line and seeing anyone that looks like me. I was tired of hearing them say, "We are all beautiful," but none of the women on the commercials looked like me.

I was tired of being politically correct and pretending race didn't matter. Because I realized that in erasing our color we are also erasing our stories. Black women, most of us, didn't grow up like white women. No shade to them but we just didn't have the same privileges and we didn't have the same burdens. No matter how much people deny it in our country, our self-esteem and self-worth is directly related to our experience of being Black in this country. The tools we use to navigate and move through the world were passed down from our mothers, from their mothers and then from their mothers, many of whom were slaves. We weren't born free or safe in this country and because education and the government and popular media have done such a wonderful job of erasing our collective story, the story of the Black woman has also been erased in many ways. But the one way it hasn't and cannot be erased is in our present-day lives and how we show up in the world. Our voice, our power, and our pain is still palpable in every corner of this world. And I believe it is time to start healing by telling our own story on our own terms and through our own lips. This is my attempt at doing just that.

In the beginning, writing this book was something of a love letter to Black women. I wanted to create something for the self-proclaimed Strong Black Woman who does too much and asks for too little. It was meant to be a handbook for my exhausted, over achieving and underappreciated sisters who make life look easy even when it's actually kicking their ass and hard as fuck. I had been doing "the work" to heal the hurt and abandoned little girl in me who never thought she was worthy of love. And while I know the healing journey is never over, I was confident that I had crossed a critical chasm and that only brighter, easier days were ahead. Girl, was I wrong.

Nothing life or death happened. It was just one of those "straw that broke the camel's back" type of situations where I was left feeling depleted, alone, and hopeless. Life had just pulled out its big old hand and slapped me right across my face and I was forced to look at some things I was avoiding. That's when I realized this book is just as much for me as it is you.

I thought I had learned these lessons of valuing and loving myself so much that I was easily able to discern harm from help. I thought I was fixed. But a series of events that left my family in more of a shambles than it had ever been I realized I had whole lot more work to do. My self-worth and value took a nose dive so fast I couldn't catch myself and before I knew it I was in a puddle of tears. I'd been doing the work for over a decade years now and I thought I had it down pat. But that experience left me feeling like the same lonely little girl who had never really been loved.

I definitely have more work to do. There are layers to this shit so it will probably be going on until I'm old and gray and doing naked yoga on a beach in Hawaii (Yes, that's where I'll be and I won't be hard to find). That's one reason why this book is such a gem. You can go back to it at any time in your life and get new jewels from it. It can be used when dealing with your family, your lover, your kids, or the folks at your job. It's more than a quick and easy read. It's a reference tool you can use to gauge your level of self-care and self-love. It's an actionable guide that has actionable steps you can take to make real and lasting changes in your life. So here are some basic tenets and givens I'll be going over in the book. I'm mentioning these now because they are non-negotiables for me and you may have to take a little time to digest them and find where they fit in your life. And trust me, if you're reading this book, they fit.

You will have to stop being so damn strong.

You're going to have to learn to be tender.

You will have to let people down.

You will have to stop trying to make sure everybody is okay.

What frightens Strong Black Women about this type of change is we instantly begin to think about how the changes we're going to make are going to affect those people around us. We've gotten it in our mind that if we don't show up on 10 all the time with all guns a-blazing, that shit is going to fall apart. The bills aren't gonna get paid. The kids won't eat. The job is going to suffer. The whole mindset has to change because you have to realize NONE of it is true. What you are sacrificing of yourself in order to accomplish what you need to accomplish is completely unnecessary and counterproductive. You're going to have to have faith in this entire process because it's a different way of looking at yourself and your life.

I also need to make two public service announcements. One, I curse, a lot. If you can't appreciate an explicit vernacular then you should stop reading now. Two, this book may trigger some painful feelings, emotions, and memories that you had tucked away. Physical, sexual, and psychological trauma are some of the reasons we have built the pseudo-protective SBW persona. You may believe that just because something is "over" that the pain of the wounds isn't still affecting you in your everyday life. You may also think that "it" wasn't that bad. Just because people didn't know any better or they were doing their best doesn't excuse their actions. Absorbing the pain doesn't do you any justice. If feelings of anger, hurt, sadness rise up while reading this book, or any other time, don't push them down. Talk with someone. Use the tools in this book. Find a therapist or counselor. Whatever you do, GET HELP! This book is all about how you can begin taking care of you so please be kind, compassionate, and patient with yourself while we're on this journey.

This book in no way takes the place of working with a professional counselor, therapist, or trained clergy. Having a professional support system is vital in this work. Unfortunately, in the black community it is reported that 63% of us believe that depression is a sign of weakness. Culturally, we experience an enormous amount of shame around mental illness. This miseducation is one of the main reasons higher numbers of untreated depression are being found in our community. This lack of attention is also why we are seeing higher rates of suicide and attempted suicide among African-Americans.

When we have a tooth ache we don't attempt to pull it out ourselves and we don't feel embarrassed for having a cavity. Instead, we go to a highly trained professional that we trust so they can help us get rid of the pain and create a prevention plan for healthy teeth. We need to practice the same logic when it comes to our mental and emotional health. I began seeing a therapist when I was a sophomore in college. I went into the nurse's office and told her I needed to talk to someone. I was raped the year before I went to college. I told two people and never spoke a word of it again. I stuffed it for as long as I could but the pain and memory of it was so alive in me that I was unraveling, hiding in the bathroom and having uncontrollable crying spells.

She put me in contact with the counselor's office and I had my first of many sessions, all of which were covered by my tuition. From there, I found a free therapy group for survivors of rape, incest, and molestation. After that, I found a licensed psychologist who worked on a sliding scale and I paid no more than $10 per session. There is help out there and it is accessible but you have to be diligent about finding it.

This book is one route. It is my love letter to myself and you. It's packed with valuable lessons it took me over twenty years to grasp. I'm still working through them and probably will be for many years. And I don't mind that because it's not a race. There is no final destination. Reclaiming our true power by loving ourselves is a life's work. It is an ever-evolving organism in and of itself. Use this book. Read it and reread it. Make notes in it. Pull out your journal and write what it brings up for you. Start difficult conversations. Use it to help you remember how important you are and how much you deserve to be happy for YOU.

# CHAPTER 2

## TIME TO LET YOUR SOUL GLOW

One of the main characteristics of a Strong Black Woman is that 99% of the time you got more shit to do than time to get it done and you don't know how to ask for help. We're working full time, going to college, cooking dinner, taking kids back and forth to sports practices, and my personal favorite, washing clothes. The tricky part about this is all this shit really does need to get done. You gotta work. The babies gotta eat. And Auntie needs your help after church on Sunday. And God forbid shit doesn't go as planned. You need to get your car fixed and now you have more bills than money at the end of the month. The stress of managing all this can make us feel alone and unsupported. We get the game fucked up when we believe that we have to do it alone or that it all has to be done perfectly. The SBW myth gets perpetuated when we pile our plates high with "To-Dos" and not enough "To-Bes." We believe our success is in our external accomplishments. So, we just keep adding things to our To Do lists. I think this happens because we haven't fully embraced and cultivated our Inner lives, our state of being. When we aren't grounded spiritually, when we don't have a strong and solid connection with our Divine nature, we drift aimlessly into a very busy life. We take on unnecessary bills, pack our schedules, and commit to doing things that don't serve us with people that don't really care about us.

Compound that with the fact that we don't know how to seek support because we believe we should be able to do it alone. All of these external things must be done because you think they must be done. Sooner or later they do need to be done, but not all of them need to be done at one time. And you have deemed that no one else is good enough to do them because no one does it as good as you do, or you don't have a support system set up where people are willing to help you do all of these things. So, you become this machine of doing. This is external and the opposite of external is internal and the opposite of doing and being. And so, a rich outer life must be balanced with a rich Inner Spiritual life. More times than not, Black women, Strong Black women, don't have that rich Inner life because there are many responsibilities that we feel we have to manage. When that happens we use all of our finite energy. Finite energy is physical and mental energy. It has a beginning and an end. That's why you get tired and exhausted. You go to sleep at night. You eat your food. Those are things that fuel the body and the brain so you can take action, but it's all finite. By the end of the day and the end of the week, you are depleted. You have more things to do than you have energy, so you continue to burn what you don't have. You continue to pour from a cup that's already empty. You haven't tapped into the rich infinite energy of your Spirit and you always come up short.

A Spiritual life is focused on being and not doing. It is one where we reconnect back to the Source of who we are. Some people call it God, Jesus. Some people find it in a church. Some people find it in a mosque. Others find it sitting Indian style on the floor in front of candle. Others find it in nature. No matter where or how you find it, it is a real thing. People experience the feeling of Source/God/Universe in many ways and on many different terms. I was raised in the church but I never had a Spiritual experience until I was in college. It came after a traumatic event and I was in deep emotional distress. I was lost, alone, and in so much pain. That was the first time I heard "The Voice."

# CHAPTER 2

In my senior year of high school I was the victim of a traumatic rape by a guy and his friend while I was out on a date with him. This was the defining experience in my life and caused me to call on a higher power like I had never done before. Daily, hourly, I begged for answers as to how this could have happened to me and begged for relief from the excruciating pain of carrying such a burden. One night, in a deep depression, I decided to take my life. I couldn't withstand the pain any longer. A voice came to me and told me how to hold on, what to do next, and how my life would be healed. It took a devastating event to put me on my Spiritual path. Before that I was only aware of and believed in things that I could see and hear with my earthly senses. Everything changed after that night.

Before my Spiritual encounter, I was only concerned with what I could prove to other people. I was preoccupied with other people's opinions of me and if I was living up to their standards. No one gave me a piece of paper with a list of what I should be. Since childhood, I adopted the implied expectations for a very Strong Black Woman. The most influential and detrimental aspect of this was wrapping my identity around the church. We were there on Sunday morning and night, on Wednesday night for Bible study, on Thursday night for prayer service and on Saturdays for ministering in the community. I was inundated with strict rules that defined me as a terrible person who needed to spend all her time repenting so she could earn her way into Heaven and not be left on Earth after the rapture.

After having religious and Spiritual experiences, I know which one holds the most power in my life. Being on a Spiritual path has lead me to some of the most non-logical forms of healing. It has allowed me to be able to live comfortably and lovingly with the past while I move forward knowing my best days are in front of me. But the Spiritual path doesn't just appear in front of you. You have to create a Spiritual life.

Creating a Spiritual life means you are ready to let go of all that you've been taught and to grab on to a deeper truth that's been brewing inside of you. More than likely you know there's something more. If you're reading this book, then you've probably had your own experience and done some studying. You know that going deeper into your soul will reveal more of who you really are and give you the answers that have escaped you by looking to the outside world. You just don't know how to get there and stay there. That's what we're going to go into now.

Building a relationship with your Spirit and putting your divine knowing into action is the greatest gift you can give yourself and those you love. The greatest! This is where you tap into your true power and learn how to align with what you want and put an end to the endless hustling and struggling to get somewhere that you don't even want to be. It is the sweetest spot of your life. Creating a vibrant Spiritual practice requires you to put yourself first. It is at the core of self-care. All of your achievements and accolades can't compare to the ability to tap into the infinite power that is you. You can only build this ability through making yourself the ultimate priority.

Turning your focus inward takes a great deal of dedication and focus. The world is always pulling at our attention and wanting us to respond to its antics. They want you to believe that your main purpose for being on Earth is to perform to their standards of being a good wife, mother, friend, employee, consumer. These are unattainable standards, so you keep striving and wondering why you never get to the mountain top. It's because it doesn't exist. If you listen to the world and society it will pull you in the opposite direction of where you should put your focus and attention.

## CHAPTER 2

So how do you go about creating a Spiritual Practice? It's quite simple. But for most of you it's not easy because it will mean you have to do something that you absolutely hate doing. NOTHING. You have to do nothing. Your inner voice is always talking to you, guiding you, soothing you but you can only hear it when you are still and quiet. I know. Let that sink in. The key to happiness is sitting your busy ass down and doing absolutely nothing. You don't have to do nothing forever, just for the first 15 minutes of everyday. It's called meditation.

Meditation is the simplest and fastest way to connect to your Soul self and begin to reenergize your life. All of your power is in the present moment. It's the only reality that exists. Humans spend over 95% of their day focusing on the past and future. The past is dead and gone. The future is only your imagination at work. There is only power in NOW. Getting in the now with meditation is a constant practice. That's why it's called a meditation practice. The most traditional form of meditation is sitting in a comfortable space on the floor or in the chair. You then use the evidence of now, your breaths to regulate your mediation. It's overwhelming how many thoughts will come racing into your mind when you sit for those 15 minutes. So much so that the thoughts will drive a lot of people to question their practice because it's too much to just sit there.

This may happen to you. If it does, it's ok. Over time you will be able to control your thoughts instead of having them control you. You will relax and from there you will learn to listen to the whisper of your soul. You will begin to understand the language through how it makes you feel. You will be guided by your truth. As you listen and carry out the tasks of your true calling, you'll get more comfortable and confident in this voice. From there you'll be led to the next steps of your spiritual journey. This is why it's so important to keep up this work. Possibly, for the first time in your life you have nothing to prove to anyone. There isn't anyone to compare to yourself. This is only about you and you.

I could try and spell out word for word how your Spiritual Practice will develop but that wouldn't do you any good. This path is personal and unique. Only you know how it will come to fruition. This is why this step is so important. You have to learn how to listen to and trust yourself. As you build your spiritual muscle, your desire to nurture and value yourself will also increase. It will create a compounding effect that you can use to support yourself in your everyday life in the most powerful ways.

A rich Spiritual life is vital to my life because it was the only thing that could help me make sense of experiences that have absolutely no logic at all, what so ever. I was a 19-year-old girl, not a woman. I was living away from home and had a strained relationship with my parents. I was broken in every way. When I look back I had been for a long time. I grew up feeling ugly and out of place. I was tall and chubby, all my clothes were second hand and I was usually the only black kid in my class and at church. My parents had a toxic and sometimes violent marriage and an even more dysfunctional and painful divorce that devastated our family in irreparable ways. I grew up feeling lonely and abandoned but masqueraded as a fun loving and outgoing girl who did well in school and people had high expectations of. For years I went through depression, promiscuity, and feeling hopeless and suicidal. It was only my Spiritual Practice that gave me the inner strength to get the help and do the work that would transform and continues to transform my life.

CHAPTER 2

# WHAT'S NEXT EXERCISE

1. Select at least three activities from the list below to begin using on a daily basis for the next 30 days.

| | |
|---|---|
| Yoga | Prayer |
| Journaling | Exercise |
| Walking | Gardening |
| Laughter | Chanting |
| Art | Chakra Clearing |
| Affirmations | Crystals Healing |
| Dancing | Energy work |

2. Make a daily schedule to create a consistent Spiritual practice. Put in in your calendar and your phone. Use reminders such as Post-It notes to put up around your house with reminders.

# CHAPTER 3

## YOU IS KIND, YOU IS SMART, YOU IS IMPORTANT

You can have on the prettiest outfit with your hair laid to the gods along with the dream career, but still believe that your life isn't worth two cents. Unfortunately, people believe that self-worth is defined by how you look to the outside world. We equate happiness with money and beauty and education. People say "What's wrong with her? She's so smart and pretty?" as if to say those two things are the recipe for a wonderful life. It doesn't make any sense when you think about it, but we believe it anyway. We work hard to have the things that will make us look happy while inside we are sad and miserable.

Unfortunately, it's a part of our programming as Strong Black Women not to value our emotions and focus on more practical and external matters such as responsibility, obligations, and reputation. When I was a little girl, my parents only wanted to know what my grades were. Why not? That's why they sent me to school. They wanted me to get good grades so I could grow up and get a good job. And once you have a good job that pays enough money to take care of all of your bills you would be complete. These are good and necessary. I understand that I'm a single mother of an adolescent boy. I believe in being book smart. I also believe in being heart smart.

Our self-worth has nothing to do with how well we do in school. It is totally independent of any conditional worth. Our self-worth is our perception of how good a person we are and how deserving we are of love. What is conditional worth exactly? Conditional worth is anything that can change or be taken away from you at any moment. It is dependent on conditions. It is a form of worth that is outside of your control because it is based on other people's perception. You can influence and even manipulate it but ultimately, you cannot control it. And it will not last forever. It will change. It will fade. It will transition. It will go away eventually.

There are two major types of conditional worth. External and Internal. External conditional worth comes in the form of money, education, looks, career, social status, etc. We work for and gain these things. They are so influential because they are the first things that people notice when they meet or see us. Every culture has their own standards of conditional worth. In America, having a Mercedes Benz is a big deal. The car turns heads because people think that a rich and powerful person is behind the wheel. It evokes admiration, awe, and jealousy. One day while watching a British television show, I saw that the metropolitan streets there are flooded with Mercedes as taxi cabs! How could something steeped in status here in the states be a such a common thing somewhere else? Then I realized that what I believed was fact - that Benzes are the shit - was conditional on location. If I lived in Britain, I wouldn't look twice at that car. Seeing that changed my perspective, helped me distance myself from conditional worth, and allowed me to detach personal value from transient things.

Internal conditional wealth is made up of one main component. That component is your behavior, and your behavior affects your reputation and personality. Your behavior drives how you show up and interact with people.

Conditional worth is powerful because it's attached to something that every person on this planet wants. Unconditional Love. There is nothing more needed or wanted than unconditional love. There is also nothing more denied. We all want this and very few of us know how to give it. It's a painful and relentless cycle. We are always in search of others to love us. When this happens we automatically go into conditional worth mode. Everyone is different so the one thing that makes one person think you are the bomb.com may irritate the next person. So, you begin to take on and exhibit whatever behavior you believe the person you want love from wants. But we want love from everyone. So, we turn ourselves into pretzels trying to win the approval, affection, attention, security, and love. And we do this by using the different forms of conditional worth. But you can't get unconditional love with conditional worth. You can only get conditional love. And conditional love, like conditional worth, is completely out of your control and will come to an end.

This anxiety and fear filled way of connecting to the world leads only to shame, disappointment, hurt, regret, and pain. It also leads to the number one reason why you can't put yourself first in your life. It leads to low self-worth. Your self-worth is the value you place on yourself as a person. It is not determined by any aspects of conditional worth. Your self-worth is how you really feel about yourself. Now you might say "Oh, I love myself." But the true measurement of how you feel about yourself is found in the choices you make in your everyday life. Do you say yes when you really want to say no? Are you afraid of asking for what you want because you fear rejection and humiliation? Are you involved in unhealthy relationships? Do you work a job you hate but refuse to do anything about it? If you answered yes to any of these questions your self-worth is being defined by conditions and therefore on the lower end of the spectrum.

The tricky part is we don't see it that way because we believe we are doing the right thing and are convinced it's going to work out in our favor one day and all the pain will be worth it. When I graduated from college I had the world at my fingertips. I graduated with honors. At 22, I already had years of work history and I lived in a thriving metropolis. But instead, diving deep into my talents and potential, I did something different. I entered into a relationship with a man doing 10 years in a federal penitentiary.

I had always had a soft spot for criminals, but this took the cake. I met him soon after I graduated from high school. He was the biggest drug dealer in the small town where I grew up and I had already suffered a traumatic sexual assault. I was estranged from my mother and barely speaking to my father. I was broken in so many pieces you needed a vacuum cleaner to pick them all up. But he didn't see that. Talk about low self-worth. I was an emotional zombie pretending to be the life of the party when deep inside I didn't think my life had any value. I couldn't see how anyone could ever love me or see any good in me. So, when he did, I crowned him the king of my heart. I was like "Hell, anyone who could care about someone as wretched as me has to be the most incredible man in the world."

Our little tryst was brief but impactful. I credited him with being a friend at a time in my life when I didn't have any. That wasn't true but I believed it was because I had shared my deepest darkest secrets with him and he didn't run away. I was void of any conditional worth or self-worth, so I didn't see how anyone could see value in me. He did and that made him a giant in my eyes. Well, you know the story. I went away to college and he went to prison. I had four years to get over him. Me and my low self-worth fell in love with another man who I thought must be amazing if he could love me, too. That did not work out (thank God). So, when I graduated, I rekindled the relationship. I spent two years talking to him on the phone while he was in jail, writing weekly letters, and making monthly 7 hour drives to visit him. You couldn't tell me that we weren't going to be together when he came home. We had plans. He told me he wanted to be with me forever. We'd get married, have babies, and live happily ever after.

All my friends knew about him. None of them discouraged me or tried to talk me out of being with him. Maybe they felt their advice would have fallen on deaf ears. They would have been correct. This went on for two years. I would occasionally date but my alliance and heart were with him. I had cut all other men out of my life so I could show him my loyalty. One weekend, I decided to surprise him with a visit for his birthday. Instead of driving down the day of the visit, I left a day early and got a hotel room. This would allow me to get there first thing in the morning so we'd have more time to spend together.

I arrived at nine am to find there was already a line formed for visitors waiting to be processed. After 30 minutes, my name was called, and I walked into the visitor's room. It was a huge room filled with round tables, each with 4 chairs. On one end was a row of vending machines. I had done this so many times that I knew to have $5 to $10 in quarters for every visit. We had lunch, drank soda, and pretended we were on a romantic date in the park instead of the cold, stark medium-security prison with armed guards. The guards kept watch for inappropriate behavior like kissing, fondling, and passing drugs, weapons, or paraphernalia.

When he walked into the room he appeared to be happy and surprised to see me. We hugged, pecked on the lips, and sat at a table. After a few minutes, we bought snacks and went outside to a picnic table for sun and fresh air. After about 45 minutes of light-hearted conversation and laughter, a woman walked up behind us and sat next to me on the wooden bench. The energy shifted. I felt it in my body and not in a good way. I looked across the table. All the life drained from R's face. His big, drooping Jay-Z lips trembled. He didn't say a word. She introduced herself to me.

"Hi, I'm … and I'm R's girlfriend."

My heart dropped. She greeted him.

"Hey," she said with a slow, southern, ghetto drawl steeped in *I got yo ass now nigga*. "I had a feeling I needed to come out here today. Something told me something wasn't right."

She let him know. The funny thing was, I also had a feeling that something wasn't right. I loved him and all, but I was beginning to wonder if things would work out the way I wanted them to. I had prayed for God to give me a sign that I couldn't ignore.

She continued.

"Did he tell you ya'll were gone get married when he got home?"

I replied, "Yes."

"He told me the same thing. He's been tellin me that since he got locked up."

When she said that it confirmed my thoughts. Her comfort level with him let me know they had known each other a long time and knew each other very well. She went on to recount the ways she knew him to confirm that her story was true. But I didn't need her to tell me that. All I had to do was look at him. His face told it all. I realized that he had been tapping his heel, vibrating the picnic table. He didn't open his mouth. He didn't speak to her. He didn't call her a liar. He didn't try to explain. He wouldn't look me in the eye. He looked past us at the trees and barbed wire fence.

"You don't have anything to say?" I angrily asked him. I could feel the humiliation causing my body heat to rise. I didn't want it to be true. This was the sign I couldn't ignore. I had fallen in love with a liar. I had believed every word. I had dedicated the last two years of time, attention, and life to a string of words carried through a phone line and worthless love letters. Without uttering a word, he put his hands on the table, stood up, stepped over the bench, turned his back, and walked into the visiting room without looking back at us. The door swung closed behind him. It was over. He was gone.

It took years for me realize that my lack of self-love caused me to attract a man who could never love me. I believed if I did enough of the right things, or used my conditional worth, that I could win his unconditional love. At the time, I never would've believed I had a self-worth issue. I thought I was undeserving of love and had to work hard to earn it. Even today, I have to correct myself from getting caught in this emotional trap.

You can't hide from low-self-worth and you can't hide it from others, either. It bleeds through every part of your life. It shows up in the ways you don't believe in yourself and it shows up in the ways you do believe in yourself. One woman may not believe that she is smart enough to accomplish something like getting a bachelor's degree. Another woman may feel confident that she can take another woman's man. Both women suffer from low self-worth. LSW is a tricky muther fucker. It can disguise itself as logic and reason. It can make a solid case with evidence that makes you believe the worst about yourself. Your self-worth creates a clear picture that can cause you to believe that you don't deserve to live. Here are a few other erroneous notions that your self-worth can cause you to believe:

You'll never find someone to love you for who you are.

You don't have anything important to say.

You aren't smart enough for that job.

You'll never lose weight.

You need to own that certain (car, purse, house) in order to be accepted.

You'll never make it.

You should give up now.

No one cares about you.

You don't matter.

What you want isn't important.

Your self-worth started developing when you were born and went home to live with your parents or the people who raised you. Each of us is valuable at birth. When we arrive in this world, our self-worth is intact. Over time, our environments and experiences shape our self-worth. If you had parents that encouraged you and held you in high regard, this would affect your self-worth in a positive way. If you were berated, abused (mentally, physically, emotionally, sexually) or made to feel less than, then your self-worth would have been negatively affected. Small things can affect your self-worth. A kid in your elementary class you don't even know may have walked up to you and said, "You're a little black crusty thing and no one's ever going to want to play with you!"

Upon hearing this, a group of kids laughs at you and walks off with the dick head who insulted you. Maybe you stood there, humiliated and defenseless. Maybe you brushed it off and pretended it didn't bother you. Either way, that experience had the power to influence the way you saw yourself for the rest of your life.

I'm telling you this so you can understand how seriously I want you to take this part of the book. If you're not willing to take a brutally honest look at your self-worth, nothing is going to change. You might as well close this book and go back to what you were doing. I assume that some things have already started to come up for you. I don't want you to play tough girl and downplay those feelings. We can't change what we don't acknowledge. I want you to take some time before reading the next chapters to take a solid assessment of your self-worth.

We all have self-worth issues. Don't compare the things you may want to work on with what someone else needs help with. Nothing can diminish your worth. As humans, we are all equally valuable and deserving of love. I don't care what you've done or what has happened to you. True self-worth cannot be diminished. I know some of you may be wondering about the murderer and the child molester. Do they deserve love, too? Yep, they do. That doesn't mean they don't deserve to be held accountable for their crimes. We are not what we do. Those are two separate things. Understanding this concept will help you separate your true self-worth from your choices based on your perceived self-worth.

If you're ever going to be able to put yourself first in your life (where you should be), then you have to establish a healthy and positive self-worth. You have to be able to look yourself in the eyes and know that you are a good person and you deserve to be happy no matter what. If you don't learn to do this, life is going to kick your ass so bad that it will make you want to fold and quit. Life is going to kick your ass anyway. It's going to put you in situations that you don't know how to get out of. It's going to create circumstances and events that leave you feeling overwhelmed, sad, and almost broken (I said almost). But with a healthy self-worth you won't ever fold. You will always have yourself as evidence that there is good in the world. That evidence will give you tenacity, compassion, and wisdom to make better choices and teach you how to creatively and successfully maneuver throughout life.

Having a college degree is a major accomplishment but it doesn't mean much if you can't get a job. You may be as gorgeous as a super model but in one second that can be taken away in a horrendous accident.

No circumstance, situation, or experience can change the fact that you are the walking embodiment and expression of God. The fact that you are alive is proof that you are worthy. You just have to believe it.

Society teaches us that as women, our value is in our pristine perfection and our untouched virtuosity. But if I crinkle and stomp on a $100 bill, it's still a one-hundred-dollar bill.

CHAPTER 3

# WHAT'S NEXT EXERCISE

Look at these areas of your life: Financial, Romantic, Professional, Family, and Physical.

1. What choices have you made from a place of loving yourself?

2. What choices have you made from a place of trying to get love and approval from others?

3. Now that you have that list, ask yourself how you felt after making those choices.

4. Name 21 positive characteristics about yourself.

5. For the next 21 days journal on one of the characteristics.

# CHAPTER 4

## GET GREEDY

When you ask for what you want it comes from a place of worthiness and belief that there's plenty to go around so you can easily get your share. Asking for what you think you can have comes from a place of lack and you not believing there's enough for you or that you don't believe you deserve to have abundance. Only one of the perspectives is useful when it comes to putting yourself first. Which one of them do you think it is?

I feel like I need to break down this whole concept of being a Strong Black Woman, so we can make some real headway. The word Strong isn't really a compliment. It's used to describe a woman who has made it her business to do more and accept less, quietly. She shows her strength by how much she can do with so little. It still pisses me off that this has become the Universal brand for Black women in this country. Why is it wrong to ask for what you want? Why don't you (or I) believe we deserve to have it? Why is it so dam hard? What are we afraid of? When I look at these questions on my computer screen, it makes me sad and mad as hell that we are still in a choke hold over asking for what we really want. It's even more maddening how much time we spend trying to make sure everyone else gets what they want.

We weren't even together three months. He was playing pool at the strip club I waitressed at when we met. He gave me a key to his house after one week. I realized quickly after that we weren't a good fit but my emotions were already attached. It went downhill fast, and it was ugly. After we broke up, we spent one last night together. That was the night my son was conceived.

As no surprise to me, he had no interest in being a father. So I took on the task of being a single mom from conception. I knew I didn't have time to whine and complain. There was an entire person growing inside of me (yikes) and I needed to make sure I was ready. Who knew babies needed so many things? I hunted for deals on second-hand cribs, strollers, and high-chairs. Then there were clothes. How could one person go through so many onesies and outgrow a cute new outfit after a single wear?

I was always buying something for him. Whatever money I had left after that went to paying bills. On the one hand, it was a relentless and exhausting cycle. On the other hand, I was in my element. I was a natural mom. I felt like I was on a mission from God, raising a Black boy. There was one thing, though. I forgot about myself.

Before my son was born, I was the epitome of young, single, and free. If I wanted it, I bought it. If I wanted to go, I hopped in my car or on a plane and went. I partied, shopped, hung out, and slept in whenever I wanted. It all came to a screeching halt when I became pregnant. My priorities shifted from carefree party girl to devoted mom who never went anywhere or did anything. Time moved so fast and there was much to do in-between working a full-time job and being a single mom. My pre-baby life was a distant memory and I didn't miss it. I partied and dated a lot. I was in my early 30's, living in one of the most successful black metropolitan cities in the country before the recession. I had my share of fun. When it was time to be a responsible adult, I didn't hesitate. I saw it as the next step. But somewhere along the way, I lost control.

# CHAPTER 4

While I was at Target shopping for my 18 month old son, I was on the phone with a close friend. I "oohed" and "ahhed" over cute baby outfits and shoes. Then, she asked me a question that made me stop in my tracks.

"Jen, you're a very good mom. You are. And you take really good care of V. But when is the last time you bought something for yourself?"

She asked as though no matter what answer I gave, it wouldn't be good enough.

"Oh, I don't know. I bought groceries and I eat groceries so that was for me."

"Jennifer, you're a good fucking mom! You don't have to prove it by not doing shit for yourself."

She let the words out as if she had held them in for a long time. She knew the pre-mom Jennifer, when we were cocktail waitresses at a popular Atlanta strip club. Back then, my hair and nails stayed DID. I had an expensive Beyoncé weave bill and drove a new luxury car (that I couldn't afford). I had a closet full of nice clothes and designer purses.

But things had changed. I was a mom and I had to be responsible for another human being. I let out a deep sigh.

"I know. I know. It's just..." I stopped mid-sentence and couldn't believe what I was about to say. "I can't. When I try and buy something for myself, my mind tallies the cost and tells me that I could be spending that money on Vincent."

"You need to buy something for yourself TODAY while you're in Target!"

For the next 30 minutes she sat on the phone with me as I sorted through racks of tanks, t-shirts, and sweaters. About halfway through I had an AH-HA moment. My frivolous and carefree lifestyle was the reason for this mess. I had been 32 years old, gallivanting in the streets, only caring about a good time, and not paying attention to what matters. Nine months later I was in the hospital having a child alone.

I didn't deserve to have what I wanted. I deserved to be punished for being irresponsible. I deserved to suffer until I learned my lesson. I didn't deserve a break or happiness. How could I? I was a statistic. I wasn't able to give my son, the love of my life, the one thing he needed most: a father. Guilt crawled through my stomach, chest and head. I stood in the women's department, my mind whirling in circles. The voice was free and it screamed at me that I was a trifling chick.

I told my friend what I thought. It took a couple trips around Target, but she helped me see things differently. She accused me of being too hard on myself. She told me that my decision to have my son despite the circumstances made me a great mom. She gave me examples so I could understand that I was a good person in addition to a wonderful mother. I rewarded myself with a cute shirt.

Wanting doesn't take away from those I love. Wanting doesn't make me an awful person. I still have desires. The more I believe I deserve what I want, the better mother, lover and friend I become. When we deny ourselves, nobody wins.

Even before I became a mom, I wasn't asking people or the Universe for what I wanted. I was existing on surface- level desires. I was only asking for what I thought I could have or what I believed I deserved. You can look like you have the world by the balls when you're barely hanging on because you're afraid to ask for what you want. You are afraid to come across as petty, childish, greedy, or selfish if you ask for your desires. You have to turn off that negative voice in your head that spreads dirty ass lies in your mind and tells you that you're not good enough.

As little girls, our first toy is usually a baby doll. Our mothers give us this doll and teach us how to take care of it. We are groomed to care for another person. On the other hand, boys are given trucks, cars, or balls that serve no other purpose than to have fun. This message weaves a thread through our lives that tells us to put others first. Asking for what you want and putting others first is an oxymoron. If I'm asking for what I want that means I can't give someone else what they want at the same time. So I have to do without or take what's left.

This is dangerous and traumatic for Black women. There's an unwritten law that this world isn't made for us. Nobody's gonna take care of you or put you first. You are part of the least important group on the planet, so you better fend for yourself. Growing up in my southern Christian home I was taught to ignore my wants and to place value on my needs. Those needs were food, clothing, shelter, education, and Jesus. Anything beyond that was vanity. Vanity was a sin and the wages of sin were death. I didn't want to die, so I carried a lot of guilt because I didn't want the life I was given. This led to conflict. I had a hard time figuring out my true values and accepting the life I wanted, even if it didn't look like the life of my mother or the other women in my family.

Since slavery, our value has been measured by our work ethic and our ability to provide and serve. We survived by being humble and subservient. The brilliance and magic of Black women and intimidated and scared white people back then.

In order to survive, we were taught to make our desire footprints small so they don't take up too much space and no one thought that we thought we were as good as the rest. This lesson persisted up through the years of the Civil Rights movement as a way to save the lives of Black women. A free woman believes she is equal to everyone else and feels entitled to what she wants. Wanting is a sign of power. It is a declaration that you are somebody, that you are here, and that you deserve to be here. Historically, it was life-threatening for a Black woman to think that way. The trauma of that mindset has been passed down through generations of Black women. It's no wonder we shrink our desires to the extent that we don't know what they are. They are buried to nonexistence within us.

You have to begin the arduous process of uncovering your desires. But before that can happen you have to believe you deserve to have them. Who do you think you are? Who are you to want this or that?

When someone one wants something, another person has to take an action to fulfill that want. To want is to exist. You deny your own existence when you deny your wants.

It feels good to ask for what you want. It's empowering and uplifting. It's scary as shit in the beginning but after that, it's a relief.

CHAPTER 4

# WHAT'S NEXT EXERCISE

1. How can you tell the difference between a true want and what society says you should want?

2. When is the last time you asked for something you wanted for yourself? What was the outcome?

3. What is something you've always wanted to do that you didn't allow yourself to do because you put someone else's needs or wants before your own?

4. What holds you back from having what you want now?

5. Why don't you believe you deserve to have what you want?

6. What do you believe will happen if you get what you want?

7. Create a turn-a-round statement from Question 5 stating why you believe you deserve to have what you want.

# CHAPTER 5

## THEY'LL BE A'IGHT

I can give you the number one reason why you are so damn tired day after day. You spend an inordinate amount of time trying to make sure people are happy with your decisions, trying to win their approval. You give too many fucks. You are trying to make sure your kids think you're a good mom. You want your parents to proud of the woman you've become. You want your boss to think you're the hardest working, most dedicated employee in the building. And you want the world to believe you're happy and have it all together. With all the mental acrobatics, no wonder you're in an unending cycle of exhaustion and frustration. You don't want to let anyone down. Your whole view of who you are is wrapped up in how everyone sees you. This an unwinnable race because you can never make everyone happy. You really can't make anyone happy.

Have you ever done so much for someone, and they don't appreciate or even recognize all you went through for them? Have you ever been a mom? That shit is aggravating. *Why the fuck did I spend all my time and money if that's the response I was going to get?* But you shouldn't be upset with them. You should be upset with yourself. First, you knew they wouldn't appreciate what you did because they rarely do, but you thought it would be different that time. Two, you had an ulterior motive for your actions. You wanted them to validate you and make you feel important. You don't realize that they're no more responsible for making you happy than you are for making them happy.

Did you get that? You've made it your responsibility for making other people happy and then decided it's their responsibility to make you happy. You know what that's called? CODEPENDENCE. I'll wash your dirty clothes and you wash mine. That way we'll never have be accountable for being dirty. And then you can be pretentious and tell yourself, "Peee-yoo! They smell way worse than me."

The upside to this is we can pretend our shit doesn't stink. The downside is we never get to experience the freedom and joy that comes with knowing you had the courage and self-love to wear the clean laundry you washed yourself. Let's be real. Nobody can clean your laundry but you. You're the only one who knows how it should feel against your skin, how it should smell, where the creases should be. When you live your life not trying to disappoint others, you miss out on the good stuff life has to offer. That growth can be tough but it's worth it when you're on the other side.

Our desire to appease people goes all the way back to the crib. Since we were infants, we've been aware of how our choices and responses affect the emotions of those we love. And back then it had very little to do with love and everything to do with survival. As babies, we were smart. We knew that those big people who attended to our every need held the key to our survival. Our primal instinct is to do whatever it takes to stay alive. We learn how to make them laugh and gasp. We learn to hold our heads up and capture their full attention. Babies have specific needs. They want to be fed, cleaned, and loved. And not in that order. Babies are geniuses. They learn quickly. "If I cry they will feed and clean me. If I cry they will soothe me and if I do things they deem special or important they will love me."

Sounds like a pretty sweet deal. The baby says, "They don't want anything from me!"

# CHAPTER 5

Little does she know that her devious and duplicitous (I mean loving and caring) parents have a little trick up their sleeve. They planned who this little baby will become. They are waiting for her to be old enough to call in on the debt, which starts around three or four for little girls. The payback for love, food, and attention is that she must do as they say and become who they want her to be. This is not intentional. Most of our parents wanted the best for us. They held our small defenseless bodies in their arms and protected us. They believed they had the best plans for our lives. And why wouldn't they?

This I scratch your back, you scratch mine continues until you're around 10 or 11 and you realize you want something different for your life than your parents want for you. I made the harsh discovery one Sunday morning right before going to church. I was in the eighth grade, living with my daddy. I wanted to be a cross between Janet Jackson in the "Pleasure Principle" video and Jody Watley on the cover of *Right On* magazine. I was just missing the weave, big hoop earnings with the key, and Jodie's black bustier. I had a pair of metallic silver penny loafers to set me apart from mere mortals. I pressed my rayon floral-print skirt with matching short-sleeved button-down shirt. I bought my outfit for picture day at school, but the outfit became a staple in my wardrobe.

It was late spring. I didn't have to worry about wearing a coat over my outfit so the entire A.M.E. Zion congregation could see me in all my glory. I walked down the hall to the kitchen where my daddy waited.

"Where you going in those shoes?" he asked me in a tone of sarcasm and disbelief.

His words stung like a slap to my face. I was heartbroken and humiliated.

"You might as well turn around and go back and change those because those ain't no church shoes. And where is your purse? A woman's supposed to carry a purse and wear stockings."

He was born in 1932 on a farm. He was trying to teach me the social etiquette he learned as a child. Things were different in the late eighties. These conflicts between us persisted. I was determined to experience the world through my own eyes. This got me in a lot of trouble and labeled me as hard-headed, bad, smart-mouthed, sassy and the most dreaded insult of all for a girl, fast. I disappointed my parents early on because I knew it was the only way I could have any autonomy. Because of these expectations, I had a strained relationship with my father until his death and still have a tense connection with my mother.

No matter how difficult it is or how much it hurts, I choose me every time. That shit feels good.

Choosing yourself is a cornerstone of putting yourself first. You will disappoint others. You will kill their expectations of you and confuse them. They need you to be that person because it validates who they are. So, when you decide to be who you really are, what does that mean about them? You flipped their boat and tipped it over. Not everyone will be happy when you become your top priority. The people who have the most to lose will give you the most push back. They will try to convince you that you're selfish and that you don't care about them, because if you did you would do what they wanted you to do. They may even remind you of all they've done for you. You can thank them and tell them they are free to do what makes them happy because you no longer need anyone for that. Others will applaud you and say, "It's about damn time!"

Keep them close. You will need them on this journey. But the most surprising group will be those who you worried about the most.

And guess what. Those are the ones who AIN'T paying you no mind. They knew that you were living a lie, but they figured you'd get it together when you got ready to. That's the wind beneath your wings group. They help you realize that putting yourself first doesn't take away from their happiness. They are your advocates and advisors.

I have been accused of being a mean, cold-hearted bitch but I'm not telling you to hurt people. Don't allow others' expectations of you to lead you to hurting yourself. Remember. If you have to choose, choose yourself. So, how do you disappoint the people you love, admire, and respect? I know. It sounds like a sick, sadistic game. I guarantee you it's not. Once you're on the other side, you'll realize how necessary it is. Chances are, you already realize this and that's why you're reading this book.

You may not have known it, but the previous chapters were the prep work for this chapter. You know what you want, you know you can have it, and you know you're worth it. You've given yourself permission and you've made a plan. You've unlearned the old lessons and have a killer support team. If you've done the work, you're ready to take action. So how do you go about putting this stratospheric principle into action? There are two routes you can take. The first is the Gangsta or Rip off the Duct Tape Method. The second is the Polite or Slowly Peel Back the Duct Tape Method.

The Gangsta or RDT Method is for women who have been trying to get their family and friends in order for a while. You've tried being polite by issuing warning after warning, but you are still at square one, trying to make everyone happy. In this scenario you have to go fast and go big. Your disappointment has to make a powerful statement. You must reintroduce yourself as a completely different person.

This serves two purposes. For one, it is a wakeup call for those you've been pacifying. Secondly, if you go big enough, you can't go back to the way things were.  If you do this, you're prepared to deal with the consequences. You're so muhfuckin tired of being tired that this is your life line. I love this route because you come out guns a blazing and make a drastic change in your life. I also know the pitfalls of this method. Ripping the Duct Tape Off Method can come from a place of deep hurt. If that is the case, then you have only sullied your intentions and made it a personal attack on someone else. If you believe you need to have a heart-to-heart conversation with a loved one about how you feel, do that before you put your disappointment plan into action. Here's an example of what it looks like in action.

"Regina, how's work being going? That's a really good job, and you should be thankful to have it."

"Yes, it has been a great opportunity, mom, but I've decided to finally pursue my true calling. And I can't do that while working this soul-sucking job. So, I put in my two weeks' notice last week."

This is what you call a double whammy. You are drawing a line in the sand with the single most influential and powerful person in your life and you are disappointing an entire department of people with one resignation letter. This is gangster for real, and yes, this is an amalgamation of several conversations my mother and I have had. By the time we get to this point, we have explained our point and tried to get people to buy into our wants but they refuse to see it our way. With RDO Method, there's no more explaining. One of my friends calls it "straight with no chaser." It's hard for them to swallow, but once they've digested it, they'll be all right. They may not like it. They may never like it, but they'll be alright.

SPBDT or Polite Method is for people who want to be gracious and take measured steps. This method is highly effective, as well, and can help you change your patterns in several different low stake areas in life. The pitfall of this approach is that it leaves you room to fall back into old habits because the changes may be subtle.

"Felicia, are you coming to dinner on Sunday? Everybody else will be there and I have some people I want you to meet." Your favorite Auntie asks.

You worked all week and Sunday is your only day to rest and do a few odd chores before the Monday rat race. What do you say?

"Auntie, I love you dearly and I appreciate the invite, but I'm not going to be able to make it this time. I'll try my best not to miss the next dinner, though."

Keep it short. Keep it simple. Keep it moving. Don't apologize or make promises you can't (or don't want to) keep. Choosing yourself is a revolutionary act of integrity. Don't abuse it. It's also a good idea to have a quick exit strategy just in case folks start trying to change your mind or guilt you into doing something you don't want to do.

Benefits of disappointing people.

You train them how to treat you.

You find out who's on your side.

You're free to live the life you want.

You become responsible for your own happiness (most powerful position everrr!)

You're here for a reason. You're here to manifest the kingdom of heaven on Earth. Why are you pussyfooting around trying not to step on anyone's toes? You were made to do mighty things. You can't do that by pandering to the folks sitting in the bleachers who refuse to live their own lives. You disappoint people by saying no when you mean no, and only saying yes when you mean yes. Once you start disappointing others by choosing to put yourself first, you raise the level of accountability for your own joy in your life. You have a responsibility to your own joy and when you stop living according to other people's standards, that joy meter just keeps rising.

CHAPTER 5

# WHAT'S NEXT EXERCISES

1. Who do you think about when you are about to make a big decision in your life? Why?

2. Whose approval have you always sought out? Why?

3. Who do you need to disappoint in order to put yourself first? Why?

4. What do you fear will happen if you disappoint them?

5. Write out your game plan for consciously disappointing them. Include a time line and what you will do if you get push back.

# CHAPTER 6

## WHO'S ON FIRST?

The quality of your life is determined by your priorities. One of the main reasons you're not putting yourself first is because your life is prioritized around two things. The first is you doing the things you have to do and the next is you doing what other people want you to do. As a SBW, you are trapped in a belief that you have to do the things other people want you to do. And when folks realize that you are acting on behalf of what is important to them, they will fill your life with ways to make themselves happy. And by the time you finish there's no room for you to do the things that are important to you. Hell, you won't even know what's really important anymore.

As a single mom, I had lumped all of my priorities around my son. When he was a baby, that was my priority. As he got older and gained more independence, I realized he still felt it was my job to do things for him that he could do for himself.

"Pick me up mommy." His five-year-old self begged as I carried six or seven grocery bags inside in one trip while balancing my purse and keys. And you know what I did. I picked his heavy ass up and carried him.

It took some exhausting nights before I started to rethink my mommy priorities. He had become accustomed to being carried. My new priority became making things easier on myself when I come home from a long day at work. The next time we came home with groceries, I gave him two lightly-filled bags to carry. I realized I could be a good mother without being a martyr.

In order to make sure you're putting yourself first, you must understand what you value. Your priorities are determined by your values, and values change over time due to circumstances and situations. When my son was a baby, I carried him because I valued his safety. When he was a little older and could walk, I carried him because I valued my time. I knew it was faster than letting him stumble behind me when I had things to do. But when he was older, and I knew he was safe and could keep up with me, my values shifted to making life easier for myself.

*Webster defines values as*

*"one's judgment of what is important in life."*

Unfortunately, if you grew up with lots of responsibilities and expectations placed on you, you never got the opportunity to do the critical self-analysis needed to come up with your own values. Or if you did know what was important to you early on, it was deemed unacceptable and you buried it. It's only normal to pick up the values of our family, peer group, culture, and the media. We are bombarded with images and notions of how we should look, what we should eat, what we should wear, what type of work we should be doing, what kind of car we should drive. The list goes on. Women on average spend more money than men on consumer goods, so we are prey for savvy advertisers. We work jobs we hate so we can pay for a car we don't like, and because the job is so stressful we stuff our mouths with food they sold us that create diseases in our body. Then they give us medicine to fix the diseases that cause more harm than good.

When you take the time to determine your own values, you can make choices that put you first. And from there, everyone else falls in line. When you make these types of choices, your life becomes vibrant and full of joy, fun, passion, and purpose.

Before you do that, you first have to give yourself the opportunity to want what you really want. Remove the boundaries and rules from your mind so you can freely explore your desires. You deserve this, girlfriend. Forget about what didn't work in the past. That was then. I used to be in relationships with men who I knew weren't good for me. And I wanted to be with them. My damaged self-esteem and low self-worth wouldn't let me believe I could have better. So, I didn't bother wanting more.

I used to think that just because I had been cheated on in the past that I was destined to be cheated on in the future. So, there was no point in wanting an honest and faithful man. I shrunk my wants down to what I thought I could have. I'll take a man that might cheat but wouldn't humiliate me, and he would always offer me financial security. Or I'd take a man who struggled with being faithful, and I would love him into not betraying me. I settled, not because I wanted to, but because I thought there was no other choice. I convinced myself that's what I wanted. I was lying. It hurt too much to want more because I was convinced I couldn't have it.

That all changed when I ended a 12 year on-and-off relationship with the man I believed was the love of my life. I wanted so badly to be with him, that I minimized all the things I wanted in a relationship so I could fit through the small emotional space he had for me. It wasn't until I got tired of the twisting myself into a pretzel in order to be with him that I ended the union for the last time. I wanted to be in a relationship that actively led to marriage, but I was afraid to want that because I didn't think I could have it. My parents had a tumultuous and toxic marriage, and I didn't know any people who were happily married at the time. I grew up in single parent home, so I wasn't raised in an environment where marriage was discussed. I figured marriage was for other people. I wasn't one of those girls who grew up imagining a white dress, a wedding day, and a Prince Charming. I wanted to have a career, wear high fashion clothes, travel the world, and make lots of money.

When my son was born, I started thinking of having a family of my own. I wanted my son to have a father. It was the missing piece to our family puzzle. But as years passed, I realized I also wanted a partner in life. I wanted someone to share my life as a parent and to grow through life with me. Becoming a parent makes you aware of time and how quickly it passes. I wanted someone who could be a witness to my life and me to his. I wanted to look back on my life and marvel over the memories we made as a family.

I didn't realize that I never allowed myself to want a traditional family because I believed girls like me didn't get chosen for those types of roles. I always thought men wanted the quiet, prissy types that didn't make too much noise and whose only goal was to attend to her husband's every need. That wasn't me. I was a woman with a past. I was intellectual and worldly with progressive views about life and relationships. I didn't think any man would want that for his wife. So, I pretended I didn't want it. It wasn't until the end of that relationship that I gave myself the freedom to allow my wants and desires to rise to the surface.

I remember sitting on the edge of my bed facing the mirror and speaking the words aloud for the first time.

"I want to be married."

The deepest sigh escaped me. It was such a relief. I was harboring shame and embarrassment for wanting to be married. After all, it was such an archaic act full of unfulfilled fantasies and naiveté. I was bigger than that. And what would all my strong and independent female friends say? We were in the "I don't really need a man," "They are more trouble than they are worth," "Just get what you can out of them," Club – AKA, The Scared, Lonely, and Hurt Club.

I didn't want to go on believing I could never really trust a man with my life, my heart, and my son. That's when I began to let go of the limiting beliefs, and started to clearly define my values and what was really important to me in a relationship. I realized it wasn't too much to ask for a man who was honest. I value deep levels of intimacy and open communication. Even though I had never had that type of relationship, I knew I wanted it. I was willing to let go of what I thought I could have so I could open the space to receive what was truly important TO ME.

If you don't decide what's important to you, then you will never ever have it. You will lead a reactionary life taking whatever comes your way. You have a responsibility to define your life on your own terms. No one has put a ring on it yet, but since becoming clear about what's important to me I started meeting a different type of man. Before, I was attracting men who weren't serious about relationships and were only interested in playing games. After I acknowledged what was important to me, I started meeting eligible bachelors - ambitious, engaging, family-centered men who were actively looking for a wife.

Getting married may or may not be your thing. That's not the point. What I want you to learn from my story is that you can never get what you want as long as you deny it. You have to be clear on your values and be willing to open yourself up, even if you're scared.

Many of our values have been determined by our past experience, our parents, friends, and culture at-large. As a child, you may have been a small-town country girl that dreamed of living in

Spain and Italy. That was my dream. I was going to be an interpreter by day, and painter and girl-about-town by night. But because all my friends were taking the traditional route after college and I was dating a guy who never even lived outside his small hometown, I shrank my dreams. I didn't have the courage to follow my dreams. I didn't believe I could have what I really wanted. I hadn't clearly defined that being in an environment that fed my sense of culture, diversity, and adventure was important to me.

After all, who was I to want so much? I was just some little black girl and I had already gained the reputation among my extended family for being loud and "fast". I was told on several occasions to sit down somewhere. By the time I got to college, I had forgotten those dreams and allowed others to shape my decisions.

I think it's easier when we put others in charge of our wants. If things don't work out, we're not responsible. We can take the coward's way out. We can blame someone else and be the helpless victim. As black women we got the martyr game on lock.

"I gave up everything so I could make you happy."

"You don't appreciate all I do for you!"

"You have no idea what I've given up for you!"

We want others to put us first and take responsibility for our happiness the same way we put others first and make their happiness our primary responsibility. Yeah, on the surface it's noble. But when you remove the layers, something else is there.

A learned behavior of manipulation and co-dependence comes to the surface. You allow others to decide what you want, and you take an inactive stance so you don't have to risk looking like a fool or making a mistake. Somewhere along the way, you decided the risk was too great. I can't bear to ask for what I really want. You spend years creating responsibilities and obligations that fill your schedule and your mind so there's not time or opportunity to slip into the blissful daydream of what you'd really like to be doing. Maybe it's hopping on a plane so you can wake up to a sunrise on the beach. Or it could be an hour in a hot, sudsy tub with no one, not one single solitary person calling your damn name or asking you for anything. I'd easily take the latter right about now.

If you don't determine what's important to you, then you can't decide what you want. And if you don't know what you want, then you will NEVER get it and you will never put yourself first in your life.

Another reason we don't want to be honest or realize what we really want is because it may mean hurting someone you love. The truth is doing what's best for you is always best for everyone else, too. They may just not realize it at the time. This fear is a powerful indicator. It can let us know who is really down for our happiness and is willing to support us. It can also be showing us who needs to removed from our life so we can be great. Either way, it is your responsibility and duty to follow the calling of your desires.

## WHAT'S NEXT EXERCISE

1. Make a list of your current priorities.

2. Make a list of priorities that reflect you putting yourself first.

3. What values must you embody in order to create these new priorities?

4. Write out a plan of how you will implement these new elements in your life, and include a timeline.

# CHAPTER 7

## YOU AIN'T THE BOSS OF ME

On the surface you look like you buck convention and blaze new paths, but a tell-tale sign of a SBW is her sense of loyalty steeped in obligation and obedience. Even if she doesn't want to do it, she will. Why? Because she was taught that it was the right thing to do, and good and respectable girls do the right thing even if it means abandoning your own self and walking to the end of the line. That sense of obedience is one of the main reasons we as Strong Black Women are so tired, frustrated, and unfulfilled. We have been trained to take orders from those that we believe know better for our lives than us. We are productive to a fault. This quote from one of my favorite books "Their Eyes Were Watching God" written in 1937 sums it up perfectly.

"So de white man throw down de load and tell de nigger man tuh pick it up. He pick it up because he have to, but he don't tote it. He hand it to his women folks. De nigger woman is de mule ud de world so fur as Ah can see."

Nanny, a former slave and Janie, the main character's grandmother, is trying to explain to her that women don't have many choices and a life of burden was almost inevitable. The mule represents someone who doesn't have the right to make their own decisions and whose job is to carry the burden of others.

Even though it's 2017, this moniker of the black woman looms like a dark shadow. If you look at when slavery and the Civil

Rights era ended, it's only a few generations old. My grandmother was born in 1919 and my mother in 1946. So, it's very easy to see how this belief system about women and their role can still have weight. Janie didn't have the authority to make the decisions for her life. Her grandmother decided that she would marry when she was only 16 or 17.

When we don't believe we have the right to have the authority over our lives, we are always waiting for someone to give us permission to be who they think we should be. They are the boss of us. And we don't feel that we can acceptably make that decision for ourselves. Not yet at least. We'll do it when we get out of our parent's house or when our kids are grown and out of the house or when we retire. We are polite and respectful, and we ask for permission to do the things we want to do. If that permission is denied by whomever we have given our power to, then we do without.

From a historical perspective, girls lived at home under their parent's rules until they married and then they lived under their husband's rules. Due to men thinking they knew everything and being intimidated by our feminine power, we were taught that we were mentally and physically inferior. So, it was only right that we waited for permission and approval from the smarter, stronger, and well-meaning people in our lives. This was at a time when women didn't have the right to work or own property or drive or even live alone. She couldn't be the boss of her own life and make decisions based on what she believed was best for her. This has made its way to 2018.

Today we can vote, drive, work anywhere we want, educate ourselves. But we shrink when it comes to giving ourselves permission to be first in our lives. We sabotage our own permission by saying, "I do give myself permission to put me first…after I finish the laundry, once the kids are sleep, after I talk to my friend who's in crisis, again, for two more hours."

I'm sorry, but that's not how it works. Somehow, asking for permission has become a trait of our femininity.

Here's where it gets tricky. To the naked eye, SBW are authoritative and take-charge. We do this at home with the kids and while at work. We make decisions that affect our children and family at home as well as at work. We've been called bossy, overbearing, sassy, feisty, and even the dreaded bitch. This "too muchness" that some people have labeled us is a smoke screen. All that RA-RA big talk is there to hide the scared little girl who's afraid to take charge of her happiness and fulfillment. She hopes that if she puts herself in charge of enough other people's happiness, someone will take the hint and look out for her. Instead, the opposite happens. Those people expect more from her and she ends up frustrated, tired, and unfulfilled. It is a vicious cycle. We have to let others be responsible for their own happiness before we have enough time and emotional energy to do the same for ourselves.

It's time for the shit to change, and it's time for it to change now. Yeah, everybody (your mama, your pastor, your husband, your community) might mean well but they don't know what's best for you. When you seek their permission, their approval or denial is only based on how your choices affect them. You have to give yourself permission to put yourself first because NO ONE can give it to you.

By the time my son was 8 or 9, I was completely exhausted as a mother, employee, and struggling entrepreneur. I was perpetually tired, but it had gotten to a place where the days, weeks, and months all ran together. I couldn't get a break. I didn't have a social life outside of reality TV and long phone conversations with my also single girlfriends.

Giving yourself permission to make your own needs and desires your priority is one of the most powerful things you can do as a Black woman. When we do this, we break a slave paradigm that has kept us chained to lives, relationships, careers, and family that don't serve our lives in a positive way. But we do it anyway. We believe if we do it long enough, someone will free us. We're waiting on someone to see how hard we've worked, how good and obedient and faithful we've been. We're waiting to be recognized and deemed worthy enough to be granted our freedom. We're waiting on someone to tell us that it's okay to follow our dreams. We're waiting on someone to tell us we're good enough. We're waiting on someone to tell us we've worked hard and long enough. We believe we need someone else to tell us it's our turn and that we deserve it. Now it's our turn to start getting what we really want.

If this is you, it is past time for you to become like Harriet Tubman and take your freedom. Tubman said she could have freed thousands more slaves, except they didn't know they were captive. Are you free? If you think you are, who freed you? Or are you living under the false guise of freedom? Have you become a well-dressed, educated, and well-paid modern slave? You may be a slave to your family's expectations. You may be a slave to the opinions of the people at church. You may be a slave to social media's standards. You may be a slave to your kids. I know one thing is for sure. If you have not given yourself permission to have what you truly want in life, you are slave to something. It's your job to figure out what or who this is.

If you told the people in your life who matter to you most, who have the most influence over your life (family, friend, boss, kids, husband) what you really wanted, would they 1.) Believe you should have it without question? Or 2.) Stop what they are doing and try and figure out how they can help you get what you want? If you answer no to either of these questions, then you're a slave to what they want.

You're working twice as hard to make sure they get what they want and waiting on them to give you the thumbs up to go get what you really want.

Don't beat yourself up. This obedience mentality for Black women is learned early on. Growing up, my parents applied more stringent rules and moral codes to me than to my brothers. I couldn't wear pants. My mama was a strict Pentecostal Christian. There was a concerted effort to make sure I was a good girl, got into Heaven, and didn't turn into a sassy-mouthed, fast-little-huzza-out-here shaming her good name.

I learned that in order to be a good person and daughter, I had to be obedient even when I disagreed. This put tremendous pressure on me. I became angry and rebellious, and ran away from home when I was 17. I spent my senior year living with my best friend and her lenient mom. Even after I graduated from college and had my own apartment and car and paid my own bills, I still felt that I needed my mother's approval to live the life I really wanted. I never got it. This was a blessing in disguise, because over the years I had to learn how to follow my intuition and stand behind what I believed was right for me.

I know you don't want to seem selfish or greedy. You don't want to stop showing up for or helping people you care about. You don't want to make people feel uncomfortable by your bright shining light or your happy- as-fuck life. Not when they're still complaining and playing the victim in their own lives. That wouldn't be right, would it? WRONG! That's exactly what the fuck you need to do. Sis, you will never be happy or fulfilled as long as you play that card. It turns you into a victim. Victims never take responsibility for their lives. They don't know how to take lemons and turn them into patron lemon drops with a sugar rim. Victims don't know how to empower their daughters and their community. If you're concerned about looking selfish or being "too much," you need to examine who you're hanging around. I guarantee they are using your value and gifts for their benefit. It's time to switch up that old tired game.

You have a right and responsibility to put yourself first and begin attracting what you really want in your life. If you don't own your life, someone else will. There is no better time than now for you to start living the life full of purpose, passion, and joy. You don't need anyone's approval. This took me a very long time to get.

I'm quirky. I don't fit into any categories. I have short, platinum blonde hair. I have multiple tattoos. I'm a single mom. I'm a visual artist and entrepreneur. Everybody in my family thought, and probably still thinks, I'm crazy. Why can't I just get a normal job, have a normal life, and go sit down somewhere? I have been all over the place, and tried and failed everything, twice. I would try one thing and soon as it wasn't working, my attention would go to the next shiny object in hopes of success. I did this with multiple businesses. I finally realized that I easily gave up on my dreams because I waited for someone's approval and permission to follow my calling. I've wanted to be a writer since I was in high school. I wrote poems, raps, short stories, essays, and started books. They sat on my bookcase or laid dormant in my laptop. This year, I finally decided to write my first book for myself without anyone's approval. Too often, we women do too much talking but not enough of taking action. We want solace, confirmation, reconfirmation, and then confirmation on the reconfirmation before we jump. This is permission seeking. We feel that if we can get others to buy into our dreams, it will be safer when we finally go for it. I realized that the only safety is in jumping and letting the Universe create your wings as you go. You fall when you wait for others to agree. You get cut and scraped by your choices. When I decided to shut my mouth and write my first book, I gained confidence in my own dreams and reassurances. Confirmations came once I gave myself permission to be a vessel for my gifts.

You are free. You can be, do, and have anything you want. You have sovereignty over your life. You have to make the decision and believe in yourself.

## WHAT'S NEXT EXERCISE

1. What are three things you'd like to do, but you haven't because you know others won't approve?

2. On a scale of 1-10, how important are each of these things?

3. Whose approval do you need the most and why?

4. What will happen if you don't get it?

5. Write a letter giving yourself permission to put yourself first. Include all the ways you will do this and reward yourself for accomplishing such a monumentally important endeavor.

# CHAPTER 8

## SQUAD GOALS

Why don't you like to ask for help? When you think about it, it seems so simple. If there's something I want or need that I can't do for myself, then I ask for help. But that's not what we do, is it? If there's something that we want or need that we can't do for ourselves, nine out of 10 times we figure out how to do it or we go without. If we really need it, we may have that one person we can ask when we need something and we ask them. By this time, we have stressed ourselves to the extent that we've caused another problem or made the original problem worse.

Somewhere along the way (slavery), we learned that we are supposed to dispense help but not receive it. This is the curse of the giver. We are taught as little girls that it is better to give than to receive, and since we always want to be better we and a lot of society took that to mean that it was bad to receive. We can't live without receiving. For every breath we give, we have to take one. It is the law of nature. The same law applies to us being able to ask for and receive help when we need it.

Being raised by a single Black woman taught me that I have to do everything by myself. I felt as if it was punishment for not having a husband. Like if you don't want to deal with the trouble that having a husband brings, then you don't deserve the benefit of his help or anyone else's for that matter. I believed it was a penance to be paid. But that penance turns into a medal of honor. Look what I can do by myself. We have a knack for turning a test into a testimony, but this one has gotten all the way out of control.

This self-sabotaging desire to be so strong that we don't need help is borne of our own pain and rejection. Malcolm X said that the black woman is the least protected creature in the world. This statement makes me sad because it is true. When we as women have been protected, it has been by men and came at the cost of giving up a part of ourselves. Sometimes, it feels like a lose-lose situation. If I do it myself, then I have autonomy over my life but I'm exhausted and alone. If I allow someone to help, then I owe someone a part of myself. It's a debt I can never pay.

When I had my son, I had guilt and shame for being a 32-year-old single mom with a trifling ass baby daddy. I thought that I had made my bed, so it was my responsibility to lie in it. Working hard and struggling was my way of proving that I was a good mother. I realized later that I was punishing myself. I only asked for help when I had no other choice. I struggled for a long time. I didn't know how to ask for what I really wanted. I never figured out my long goal. I focused on day-to-day survival. A decade passed before I was forced to ask for help. I was jobless, carless, and me and my son were sleeping on a cot in a church office with all our belongings in Rubbermaid tubs. And that was the good part. I met a group of people that were so kind and loving. They didn't judge me for being an educated woman with lots of experience who couldn't seem to keep a job or take care of her own child. They saw someone who needed help. That's it. Through that experience, I learned that being hard on myself kept me from getting ahead in life. Asking for support does not make me a horrible person that should be ashamed of myself. I don't run out of chances to deserve support because I will need it for the rest of my life.

If we are going to put ourselves first and start a serious regiment of self-care, we need a solid support system. Longtime friends that I now call my sisters helped me in my time of need. Others were complete strangers that I refer to as my angels. Each group is priceless. You need both. Look at the world as your support system. Even though we feel like we are alone, we are not islands. Our interconnectivity holds all of us up.

Dispel the myth of the Strong Black Woman, not needing help, and thinking you can do it all by yourself. Be so smooth at enlisting support and getting the help that you need that it becomes second nature. I know it may seem daunting but look at it like your Ask Muscle. Get your mind out of the gutter! I said Ask. But they have some similarities. They're both tight! And you usually only use them when you have to. I want you to start to exercise your Ask Muscle. That's the only way it will get stronger.

It is our natural birthright to be happy. Babies are born believing they should have all their needs met. That's why they scream bloody murder when they don't get their way. We're supposed to have time for ourselves. We're supposed to be supported. But can't nobody support if you don't let them know that you need help. And that's the hardest part about being a Strong Black Woman.

When we have this emotionally destructive mindset, and we feel sad and depressed and angry and tired, we just think that's just the way it is. No, that is our energy, that is our body, that is our spirit, telling us that we need to make another choice. We need help.

It's not natural to feel bad. It's not natural to feel alone. It's not okay to believe that we don't deserve support. It doesn't make any sense. When you start to ask for help and support on a regular basis, you will learn that there are people that you can trust. There are people who want to help you and who don't want anything back from you, except to see you happy and well. What you can learn from asking for help is that you are valuable and that you are loved just for being alive. You are not here to earn love and approval by going it alone.

When you ask for help, you learn that you're not alone. You learn that you are loved and you are supported. When you ask for help, you learn that the expectations you have for yourself are unrealistic. You learn that you have more flexibility in life than you know.

I get it. You've opened yourself up. You've trusted people and they let you down. Maybe you were betrayed by someone you loved. I know what that feels like. It hurts like a muthafucka and makes you not want to need anyone ever again. You decide that you're the only one who has your back and you're the only one you can trust. Sounds good. But deep down inside you wish you could lean on someone when you get tired. You yearn for someone to hold your burden so you can rest. You wonder what it would be like to have someone there to call who you don't have to worry about them taking more than they give. You just want to be on the receiving end more than you are on the giving end. You can have the experience of being supported but you have to learn how to ask and who to ask.

Let's be clear. Everyone can't be on your support team. Some people don't mean you any good. Others want to be there for you, but genuinely don't know how. Building a support system is like going shopping. You have to know what you're looking for and you may have to try on more than one thing in order to find the right fit. In order to put together the most effective support system, you have to know what areas of your life you need the most help with. Number one on my list is child care. I need to know I have at least three people I can call when I need a sitter. For almost 5 years, I only used a sitter when I had to work. Other than that, my son was with me. It wasn't until I decided I wanted to start going out and dating that I was able to start asking for help and trusting people with my most precious commodity.

Your support system is not a place to emotionally dump. It's a tight knit crew of people who have proven that they want the best for you and have skill sets and resources that you lack. Do you need an affordable and knowledgeable mechanic so you can stop getting robbed at the dealership? Make a few calls. Ask for recommendations on Facebook. Sometimes your support system can be virtual. Being available to receive help doesn't mean you have to spill your guts and tell all your business. It just means you have to learn how to ask.

When I moved into my house after being homeless for a short time, my son and I slept on air mattresses because we didn't have one stitch of furniture. The clothes that didn't go in the closet stayed neatly folded in our suitcases day after day. I was so happy for us to be in our own place after almost 3 months of bouncing around from place to place, that I wasn't even thinking about furniture. That lasted for about a week. I wanted to be able to walk into my room and climb in my bed, not fall onto an inflatable bed. Because I had been humbled by experience of being homeless taught me the fine art of asking for what I need and seeing what happened.

Without over thinking it I picked up the phone and called a good friend. I asked her if she knew anyone who might be giving some furniture away or had some for sale for cheap. Come to find out, a mutual friend was cleaning out her storage and needed to get rid of almost an entire house full of furniture on the same day I was calling! To make the miracle even more amazing, her storage shed was less than three miles from my house. By the end of the day I had two, almost new bedroom sets, living room and dining room furniture completely moved into my new home. It all happened because instead of feeling shame for not having any furniture I felt deserving of having some. That shift made all the difference in my life. And the kicker is two weeks later another friend called me and told me her sister was trying to empty her storage of unneeded furniture, décor and kitchen items. I could have what I wanted as long as I could come pick everything up. So in less than one month I went from a completely empty house to a fully furnished home with more things that I could possibly use. That's the power of a support system and being able to receive the help when you need it.

Not asking for help is selfish. You are denying someone the opportunity to do something for you. Them helping you also feeds them. So, don't take that away from people.

Not asking is also disrespectful, and sends a negative energy message. You have decided that others aren't able to help you. You are seeing them in lack and limitation, not in the fullness of who they are. Remember, they are also the original embodiment of God. They are capable of great and mighty things. One of those things might be helping your stubborn butt.

That would just open us up to be disappointed. That would mean that someone else would know that we don't know everything. That would lead us to the conclusion that we are not an island and we don't want to be in a vulnerable place, needing somebody else.

Two or three people disappoint us in childhood and it impacted us. So, now we can't count on no damn body. So, we're going to do it all ourselves.

I think in the end, SBW don't build strong support systems because we don't believe we deserve it. And we think that us needing help makes us useless because our only value is in doing everything and being there for everyone.

We think our value is in being so strong, mentally strong, emotionally strong, and physically strong. It's not fucking true. It's not true based on the way we feel when we abandon ourselves and refuse to ask for help.

So, the value aspect really goes back to the childhood trauma. This goes back to us believing we had to earn love. And we have to earn this love by doing. Many of us had to be way too self-sufficient, way too early. And that was what kept peace in the house. That is how we contributed and it was necessary at times.

Yeah, we are stubborn as fuck. And everybody knows you're stubborn and you'll go down fighting with that stubbornness. You let it drive you to diabetes, migraines, arguments, and bad blood, all because you refuse to let people love on you. We are not meant to live as islands. When we are vulnerable enough to create a community around us, we can't help but nourished and rise to new heights.

As we grow to value ourselves, we begin to let ourselves off the hook and realize we're not supposed to do it alone. The unrealistic expectation that makes us walk around with our cape on starts to fade. In its place is more understanding and compassion for our journey.

## WHAT'S NEXT EXERCISE

1. Make a list of 10 people you know that want to see you win.

2. What keeps you from building a strong or stronger support system in your life?

3. What areas of your life do you need the most support with?

4. List at least 5 organizations, groups and or businesses you can reach out to in-order to get a higher level of support for increasing your self-care?

5. Call or email everyone you listed here. Tell them what you need and ask how they can support you.

# CHAPTER 9

## FAILING TO PLAN IS PLANNING TO FAIL

When people are serious about accomplishing something substantial, the first thing they do is make a plan. Now if you are doing what you've always done, then you don't need a plan because the steps are then in your muscle memory. You can do them without effort or thought. But when you attempt to do something that is outside your norm, you need focus on a different skill set than you are used to. You need a plan. We use plans every day for all sorts of things and they are helpful. If you want to cook something new, you go on Pinterest and look up a recipe. A recipe is just a plan. It tells you everything you need to do and have to create a delicious meal. When you attend a new class, the teacher hands out a syllabus. That syllabus is the plan for how the class will go, what you will need to do, and what you need to learn in order to pass that class.

When you enter an address in your GPS, it gives you a plan in the form of directions with route options and estimated arrival times. Plans are powerful when we are trying to accomplish a goal. Imagine trying to bake a cake for the first time with no recipe. You wouldn't know where to start, and you'd end up with a nasty burned bread. If you get in your car and start driving without knowing when to turn left or right, you'll drive in circles, get lost, and run out of gas.

The best plans are very special. They are written. Has someone told you a recipe or given you verbal directions? That is the most confusing shit, especially if you're directionally-challenged. I have gotten lost walking around the mall. Before cell phones, I printed

Yahoo directions to every place. After a while, I'd have a pile of Yahoo directions in my glove compartment.

A wise woman told me that if it's not written down, it doesn't count. There's power in writing your desires and intentions on paper. Statistically, written plans have a higher chance of being achieved. Write it down and make it plain.

Now that you've gone through all the chapters, it's time to make a plan for putting yourself first. It's all fun and games when you're just flipping pages and imagining how your life would be if you decided to change the game, shake things up, and live for yourself. It's another story when you have to step outside of your comfort zone, create new habits, and take risks. It's easy to find a way to out of taking action or water down our intentions. That's why this chapter is VITAL.

We're going to make a plan with a clear objective, tools, and a timeline. This plan is valuable because it tracks your progress and helps keep you committed to what you want in life. I want you to stay focused without becoming overwhelmed. This chapter is about taking everything you've learned and doing the damn thing.

I want you to see what if feels like to start pouring into yourself. You do so much for others. You cater to the smallest details and take into account the feelings of your mama, husband, kids, friends, boss, and everyone else. You do mental work for everyone except yourself. Somewhere along the way, you decided you could wait or you didn't need all that attention. When we took the focus off of ourselves, our lives stopped being deliberate. We became anchorless in our ambitions and dreams. We're blown with the wind and the rains of life, with no real control over the paths of our lives.

It doesn't have to be this way. But you're the only one who can change it. The simple act of creating this plan together is an act of putting yourself first. It is a declaration to yourself and to the Universe that you are dedicated to your own happiness. You are telling yourself that you deserve to be a priority in your own life. This plan is a gift to yourself. You deserve it.

Have you thought about what putting yourself first looks like? Which part of your life do you want to change first? You may need to make changes in every area. Prioritize this plan so you can finish what you start, and do so at a high level. This is conscious Soul work. It ain't for punks. It's for women who realize that their strength is in becoming more in-tune with themselves and understanding the value of loving themselves. When we do this, the family, the career, the community, and the world benefits. This is the most important work you can do. Set yourself up for nothing but success. #Wethebest.

## WHAT'S NEXT EXERCISE

1. How do you decide which area of your life needs immediate attention? Which area is causing you the most pain?

Circle one: Health Career Family Romance Community (school, church, civic organizations, etc.)

2. Describe what's going on and why you believe you need to work in this area first.

3. Close your eyes. Take a few deep breaths. Write the perfect way your plan can work.

4. Now write about WHY this is important to you at this time in your life.

5. What type of support do you need in order to carry out this plan? (Refer to the last chapter)

6. What type of tools will help you? Write what you come up with and how you'll us these tools.

*Here are some options. You may come up with your own ideas, too. A journal is a powerful tool to help you write your feelings and thoughts if you become anxious or frustrated. It's also valuable for writing the different parts of you plan as you make progress. Your phone is another super-hero tool. Use the alarm and calendar apps to set reminders for you to do things like repeating affirmations. You can set a reminder in your phone to ask for help or to say no or to remind you of why you're doing this.*

1. Who do you believe you'll have the most push back from and how are you going to handle them? Form a place of self-love and self-respect while also being true to your new mission.

*Remember - Making a plan and writing it down signifies that you are taking yourself seriously. Not writing it down is just another form of self-sabotage. We make list for groceries, budgets, and Christmas gifts, but we won't make a list of how we can stop being strong for everyone and put ourselves first. Stay accountable and focused.*

# CHAPTER 10

## THROW OUT THE RULE BOOK

You have value and you deserve to be first in YOUR life. You don't deserve to be first because of what you do or have or what you've accomplished. You deserve to be first because you want to be first and you deserve it just by being alive. You deserve to see yourself as the priceless being you are. This can only happen when you commit yourself to being a priority in your own life. It's time for everyone else to get in line behind you.

This may seem like a strange way to think, but your Soul has been telling you this all along. You just haven't been able to hear or understand the voice. That has changed. Maya Angelou said, "Now that I know better, I do better."

We've been taught over the centuries through example and instruction to put ourselves behind everyone. We have not been trusted with authority over our lives. We have allowed others to tell us what is best. For too long, the priority has been to do for others and neglect ourselves. We were rewarded with a crown and called Strong. Little did we know that crown was filled with thorns. For hundreds of years we've pretended to be grateful for that painful gift. That era is gone. A new one has emerged in its place.

With the tools in this book you have the opportunity to change the course of your life. You can live a full and empowered life full of joy, passion, and purpose. You can access your power. Guess what? When you do this and do it consistently, everyone around you will benefit. The world will be better for it. Black women make the world go round. We always have. We have raised the children, worked the field, supported the men, and taken a stand. We have defended our families and communities against transgressions and terror. Yes, we've had to be strong in the past. Now it's time for us to realign our power and nurture ourselves the way we have always nurtured others.

Your life will change to the degree that you implement this book. I hope you're convinced that you deserve to be at the front of the line in your life. When you put you first, other people will put you first. It's such a magical time to be a Black Woman today. We have more opportunities than ever before. Black women between the ages of 30-45 are the most sought after marketing demographic in America. We lead the way in becoming entrepreneurs. We are graduating with advanced degrees in record numbers. Black Girl Magic is real. But we can't let it be the prize at the expense of our true happiness.

As you practice these principles, be kind to yourself. Practice massive patience and self-compassion. If you stumble, rest there for a moment until you're ready to get up and ask for help. Let people see you in the midst of your transformation. Let them see you in all your colors. Give yourself permission to be hurt, sad, confused, vulnerable, tender, and soft. They are all you. We can be hard on others, but we are brutal with ourselves. This is not the time for that. Love yourself and get reacquainted with your desires. Learn how to be more and do less. It's time for you to move out of the struggle hustle. Move into the effortless flow of life that comes from being selfish…I mean self-full.

Books, videos, and resources for self-care and putting yourself first will fall in your lap just when you need them. I'm always here and will continue to pour into you. This is a journey we take together. I will not leave you. We're in this for the long haul. I will continue to provide tools and inspiration, sharing my story in hopes that it will resonate with you. Keep doing the most important work you will ever do, which is to love yourself more and more. You have never been in this by yourself and you never will be.

## WHAT'S NEXT EXERCISE

1. What part of this book are you going to implement first? How?

2. Name 5 ways you practice self-compassion and tenderness as you embark on this journey?

3. Write a love letter to yourself detailing why you deserve to put yourself first and how you promise to do whatever it takes to make it happen.

Printed in Great Britain
by Amazon

45826807R00051